Reality Rule

by

P O Richards

Published by: P O Richards

© Copyright 2004
P O Richards

The right of P O Richards to be identified as the author of
this work has been asserted by him in accordance with
the Copyright, Designs and
Patents Act 1988.

ISBN :0-9548981-0-9

First published in 2004

Printed by:
ProPrint, Riverside Cottages, Old Great North Road
Stibbington, Cambs. PE8 6LR

Reality Rule

The Author's Note

Jamaica Clarendon where I stood,
Inside my kitchen cooking some food.
It was an early Wednesday night,
Off went the electric light,
On came this spiritual insight,
Which had inspired me to write,
For I have spent no time in college,
Some one had given me this knowledge.
I know not from whence it came,
But always burning like a flame.

From
P.O. Richards
(ABDULLAH)

TO MUSHTAQ AHMED
with Best wishes.

Contents

Mission Accomplished

This African has made a sincere vow,
To no mortal would he bow,
He had kept that vow right up to now,
For apartheid surely did cause a row.
He was born with this determination,
Freedom, justice, for his entire nation.
The world had come to realise,
This man would never compromise,
So power could not come by surprise.
Imprisoned and suffered in every manner,
But he held firm onto his banner,
Death would come before dishonour.

His patience, fidelity, integrity, zeal,
Calmness of mind, self discipline,
Cool courage, devotion, earnestness and principle,
Had made him, this century, one of this kind,
Hatred and vengeance, he had left behind.
Forgiveness and love is in his heart,
This he had right from the start.

A cleansed and chosen vessel is he,
He's here for all the world to see.
A true leader he was born to be,
For God told him, go, set my people free.
He had answered his master's call
It's freedom now for one and all.
Through him, apartheid is now relinquished,
At last his mission has been accomplished.

All that I have said is true,
Mr Nelson Mandela, this noble character is you.
For you are blest above the rest.
and with your knowledge so unique,
More than any tongue can speak.

Blood Baths

Blood Bath is here, there, everywhere,
We can see it very clear,
Those who cannot see, can hear,
They just kill and do not care,
And caused a lot to live in fear.
The first, they say was done by Cain,
Since then it's like the falling rain.

From ancient history we were told,
About those wicked men of old.
There were four kings of Palestine,
They never could be friends of mine.
Herod The Great massacred the innocent young males,
And spared all the young females.
For he heard of a new born King,
A competition this would bring.
Herod Antipas had claimed John the Baptist's head,
For the things that he had said.
Herod Agrippa first, put the apostle James to death,
But never could he blow one breath.

Saint Paul met Agrippa second, face to face,
But also dropped out of the race,
Their victims couldn't stand the pace.
They were known as Kings of the Jews,
But they were also bad news.
Rome was those two Emperors home,
Where blood baths never ceased to roam.
Caligula, for his cruelty and vice,
Didn't seem to be very nice.
Nero was the one with a mad head,
He loved to see the colour red,
I had to name him old time dread,
For many Christians blood were shed,
That's how his hungry lions were fed.
His hand picked women stayed by his side,
While men were forced to commit suicide.
He played his harp while Rome on fire,
Blood was what he did require.

There were some crafty cruel raiders,
They were called the Christian Crusaders.
Jerusalem the Holy Land, sacred to you and me,
But when their expedition went to sea,
Blood, more than the Sea of Galilee.
Men burnt alive for heretic views,
Surely couldn't be good news,
Or death that any one would choose.
Stomachs ripped open, searching for gold,
By some blood thirsty men of old.

Rivers of blood when men were slaves,
Not even Jesus' blood could save,
Neither the coward nor the brave.
No matter how loud those preachers shout,
Blood redemption won't work out.
Repentance is the only way,
My sins can be washed away.

Genghis Khan conquered a vast empire,
With blood just like a vampire.
Throughout the African continent,
There was always discontent.
When the missionaries came with bible and gun,
The natives thought this would be fun,
But before the day was done,
Africans' blood began to run.
The river Nile flows very far,
Also blood from tribal war.
To kill was all the skill they knew,
They thought of nothing else to do.

Blood has left so many scars,
From those Napoleonic wars.
Also the British, French and Russian Revolution,
Blood baths were the main solution.
And during the Crimean War, four nations blood ran
like a car.
Ivan The Terrible, Peter The Great,
Two Russian tsars of blood and hate.

The American Indians were like the sand,
But were eliminated from their land.
Blood was the strongest defence,
That won the War of Independence.
And when the Civil War was done, blood was how
the West was won
Now they can't live without the gun.

How World War One had started,
The Austrian Arch Duke Franz Ferdinand was
assassinated.
World War Two was by Adolf Hitler,
A fascist Austrian Dictator.
Throughout World War One and Two,
Oceans of blood those ships sailed through.
Also in two the Japanese turned blue,
For those two nuclear bombs were new.
Hitler controlled millions of Jews,
Blood was how they paid their dues,
For he gave them no chance to choose.

The Vietnam War ended in this manner,
Blood shall flow before dishonour.
The Iran Iraqi War was nothing new,
For nearly nine years, blood kept flowing,
Through and through.
But Desert Storm was worse than Hell,
For within a shorter spell,
More bombs and blood than tongue could tell.
The Bosnian blood baths was another Hell,
Where many thousand Muslims fell.

There was September Eleventh atrocity,
In Washington and New York City,
Blood baths from terrorists' activity,
Which had ignited America's wrath,
And caused Afghanistan that blood bath.
Then another blood bath of vast destruction,
Descended upon the Iraqi nation.
By our world power combination,
But this blood bath is still in motion,
Which is causing some commotion.
But this Middle East road map for peace,
May cause that blood bath to decrease.

Thou shall not kill, the good book said,
But some say Jesus' blood was shed.
Blood baths always taking innocent lives,
With bombs, guns, machetes and knives.
This has caused so much confusion,
I had to come to this conclusion.
No one on earth can convince me,
That blood baths could ever ransom me.

The Mystery

This world could be ten billion years old,
Her true age can never be told.
If we were really made from clay,
What on earth else could I say?
Who knew the time when they were born?
Night, day, evening, or early morn?
We may believe what we were told,
But some don't live till they grow old.
Time and space, no one can trace.
On these subjects some scientists do lecture,
But each one's theory could be mere conjecture.

The sun, the moon, the starry skies,
We see them with our naked eyes.
The different kinds of fruits and trees,
The Mystery of the deep blue seas.
People of all different races,
Living in many different places.
With their different ways and minds,
Animals, insects, birds, Plants, fishes of all kinds.
The rain, the rivers and the springs,
And underground are other things.
Such vast amount, no one could count.
This portion of the mystery of creation,
We are all witnesses to her duration.

All who had died throughout those years,
Never a whisper in our ears.
Although we shed so many tears.

This, I would really like to know,
When death came in, where did life go?
The prophets, Elijah, Elisha, Jesus, could raise the dead,
According to what the bible said,
But they have all gone on ahead,
Some say that we were misled.
An open mind to what I've read.
Great people like Pythagoras, Socrates, Plato,
Aristotle, Nostradamus and the rest,
Not one of them could stand the test.
The creation of mankind is a mystery,
Far greater than our petty artistry.
This mystery was before all history.

We can't touch the sun, nor reach a star,
No matter how clever we say we are.
This mystery is not a man made toy,
Nor was created for us to destroy,
But for all creatures to enjoy.
In spite of all these human inventions,
And also our future intentions,
Mixed with all kinds of contentions,
This mystery is beyond human comprehension.

The Drug Heads

I was born and raised down Memory Lane,
But never seen heroin, crack or cocaine.
I remembered listening to the news,
Which was based on drug abuse.
They mentioned use abuse, refuse,
They also mentioned no excuse.
But what made me so confused
They say that it can blow your fuse.
So drugs can't be a friend to choose.
I left and went into research,
Which did not leave me in the lurch.

When heroin, crack and cocaine,
Starts to terrorize the brain,
It can drive anyone insane.
Some got themselves injected,
and ended up infected.
Once you become hooked on heroin,
You're destined for the rubbish bin,
A war that no weak heart can win,
Take my advice and give it in.

The craving that the addicts feel,
Causes lots of them to steal.
When some girls become destitute,
Drugs turns them into prostitutes.
Some can't afford to buy the drugs,
And that's what turns them into thugs.

They never have enough to share
And when they're high,
They have no fear,
None users always should beware,
For drug heads never seem to care.
When drugs take control of the head,
They become the living dead.
I don't want to see that stuff,
To hear about it is enough.
From drugs I always will refrain,
For I'm not going down the drain,
And I'm not leaving memory lane.

The University

This world is an open university,
With opportunities and adversity.
We can learn, earn and sometimes burn,
When situations become stern,
Some don't know which way to turn,
While many of us show no concern.
Not all of us are well educated,
But all sometimes get complicated.

This road I'm on, is rough and tough,
I proclaimed "I've had enough!"
But when I stopped and looked around,
I saw people lying on the ground,
With no strength to make a sound.

I hid myself from desperation,
And shouted aloud to determination,
Please help me reach my destination.

We parents are like vehicles,
We transported our children here,
But when the journey is complete,
And they can stand on their own feet.
Some refused to pay their fares,
While some end up shedding tears.
Some say to parents, "we don't care,
Who asked you to bring us here?"
Some parents have to grin and bear,
It causes some to live in fear,
While some are plunged into despair.
But I pretend I cannot hear,
For the boomerang will soon reappear.

Some take charge of the driving seat,
And ask their parents to retreat.
These are the ones who are discreet,
Will sometimes wash their parents' feet,
And make sure they have lots to eat,
Also look decent on the street.
These shall escape adversity,
In this open university.

The Viper

I don't know from whence Aids came,
So there's no one that I can blame.
Both sexually transmitted and through blood
transfusion,
Causing whole sale deaths and much more
confusion.
Bare back sex is a thrilling ride,
But that thrill for millions was suicide,
For victims have nowhere to hide.
To avoid this sneaking viper snake,
You should always keep awake,
For Aids he gives and lives he takes,
The thoughts of dying gives the shakes.
And no sniper can eliminate this viper.
Some say, if they had it they wouldn't care,
We have to die sometime, somewhere,
But if I had it, I would fear,
Spreading HIV everywhere.
For Aids is not something to share,
No other virus can compare.

Before bare sex, both should be tested,
To be sure they're not infected.
If you wish to have sex at random,
Make sure that you wear a condom.
Sex should be a sacred thing,
Not for sale, nor just one fling.

It's sex why we are here,
Why should Aids put us elsewhere?
This is what I know for sure,
Aids don't come knocking on my door,
If you want to hear the score,
Prevention is the only cure.

Terrorism

I have heard the story told,
Of Samson the strongest man of old.
His hair was kept at a certain length.
For in it he had all his strength.
He was a famous Israelite judge,
But for his strength the Philistines
Had a grudge.

A woman named Delilah in which he did confide,
Tricked him and took him for a ride.
She kissed poor Samson and scratched his head,
And came up much closer on the bed,
Imagine what they did and said,
But when he fell asleep,
His enemies shaved his head.
They also took his sight,
That surely was an awful fright.
When his hair grew again,
His strength came back,
And he came with a vicious suicidal attack,
Which knocked the Philistines off their track.
Was this the very first terrorist attack?

I am not a judge nor jury,
But the Philistines did set fire to fury.
For they suppressed equal rights and justice,
To practice oppression and injustice.
Samson and this recall,
should be a lesson to one and all.
Never you trust a pretty face,
It may bring you a sad disgrace.
Delilah found out what she wanted to know,
But Samson and many Philistines had to go.
That was only just to show,
We shall all reap what we sow.

The Tongue

The tongue can make such eloquent speech,
Without the tongue we couldn't teach,
Nor could any doctrine preach,
Or any conclusion reach.
Sometimes when we join and sing,
Such sweet harmonious sound it bring.
The tongue helps us to fall in love,
And communicate with our heavenly father above.
But sometimes it becomes obscene,
And needs some scrubbing to be clean.
We use it sometimes to advertise,
Emphasize, criticize, chastise and give advice.
But some use it to tell lies,
And pretend to be wise.
Millions use it just to spite,
And also to cause a fight.

It can cut sharper than a knife,
The tongue can make you lose your life

We also use it to backbite,
Although we knew it wasn't right.
It can sting worse than an adder,
When it's used to abuse each other.
A tongue which is allowed to roll,
Will always get out of control.
The wound of the blade may one day heal,
But the wound of the tongue you'll always feel.
So whether you are old or young,
Control the language of your tongue,
For many already have been stung.

My Love

When life returns from whence it came,
My love will forever be the same.
I don't wish to tell a lie,
How can true love ever die?
When infatuation passeth by,
Broken hearts begin to cry,
For they thought love was drawing nigh,
But it was just an awful sigh.

My love is earnest, it is real,
It's something you will surely feel,
If your love is also real.
It is not just like a meal,

or like a spinning wheel,
This is a love no one can steal,
Or even try to make a deal.
It's like four seasons of the year,
To hear, bear, care and share,
This is my true love affair.

My love didn't come by chance,
Nor by just a mere romance,
It cannot fall into a trance.

My love is one that grows and flows,
To love and cherish those who knows.
This love of mine will always shine,
Night and day, I hope and pray,
My love will be here to stay.

'Mars' 'Ares'

This world must know what is my worth,
I'll clean no mess I've made on earth.
I shall continue to contaminate,
For many I underestimate,
Except few close friends, and my best mate.
Terrorism is what I love to hate,
Terrorists, I will not tolerate,
The lot I shall eliminate.
And leave things in a horrible state.
A new heaven and earth, I shall create,
And some day I may procreate,
But that will surely have to wait,

I've got no time to set a date.

I have to go up now on haste
I'm leaving all my nuclear waste.
I invented weapons of mass destruction,
I've got all kinds in mass production,
On Mars I'll start a new construction,
And I shall give my own instruction.
I have now got a different intention,
For those already in detention.
And those who won't do as they were told,
I shall knock them out stone cold.
I'm working on this new invention,
Which will attract the world attention,
But it may cause some contention.

When I control the universe,
I'll plunge those terrorist thugs into reverse,
Of human beings, they are the worse,
On them I have pronounced a curse.
I don't want to hear of Aids nor SARS,
I'll take my cars to drive on Mars,
And fight some wars above the stars,
For I am God of all wars.

My Happy Home

Jamaica is my happy home,
Where freedom never cease to roam.
Food, fruits, flowers of all kinds grow,
Lovely sunshine with its glow,
No room here for frost or snow.
White sand beaches by the sea,
That's a lovely sight to see.
Fragrance from the healthy breeze,
Makes me relax with ample ease,
I can do just what I please.

The Dunns River with its fall,
We can always have a ball,
The Rio Grande, we can sprawl.
The River Cobre silent, looks asleep,
But many it has caused to weep.
Though our island look so small,
You name it, we have got it all.

Gazing at the starry skies,
Seems to brighten up my eyes.
The cluster stars, they are a sight,
Always twinkling through the night.
The full moon gives a special light,
I can see right through the night.
The flying insects with their lights,
They see through the darkest nights.

The cocks crow just before dawn,
Saying it's the birth of morn.
I love to hear the birds that sing,
Such sweet melodious sound they bring.
But crickets are such noisy things,
They could never learn to sing.

Even the animals are free,
They walked the towns like you and me.
Winter sometimes look like spring,
So fresh and green is everything.
Our forests with their lumber trees,
Sometimes they whistle with the breeze.
At times we get a little storm,
Which always does a little harm,
But soon it turns into a calm.

The countryside is where I live,
We receive and sometimes give.
I always work my little farm,
For my home is always warm.
I would like the world to know,
No one here on earth I owe,
That's why I'm free to come and go,
And surely this is what I know,
If God had made a better place,
He's kept it for himself in space,
So anywhere on earth I roam,
Jamaica is my happy home.

The Head

We were given just one head,
To use and get our daily bread,
I did not want to be misled,
That's why I did my thing instead,
I choose the way I want to tread,
When I feel tired I go to bed.
For some people tried to control my brain,
But from that life I did refrain,
For that was driving me insane.

I had to work and watch the clock,
I was like a sheep into a flock,
On every door I had to knock,
My thoughts became as hard as rock.
I wasn't very bold,
I had to do what I was told,
I knew that I was getting old,
In winter I was very cold,
That lifestyle I could not uphold.

I used my head to get away,
But in that land I wouldn't stay,
I went down on my knees and say,
Heavenly Father, please help me to
Reach home safe one day.

Our Father surely did answer my prayer,
For I was taken out of the mire,
That was what I did require,
Soon after I did retire,
Now I've got my real desire.

Oppression

Oppression is what the world should hate,
For endless evils it does create,
I don't know what is my fate,
But I will never co-operate.
For there are some despotic men,
Their country is like the lions den.
I'm not too keen on living there,
For tyrants I shall never fear.
They used their might to conquer right,
And that must surely cause a fight.
We know that they don't really care,
Their people have a lot to bear.
But time will take such gentle care,
In the end they'll get their share.

If tyranny do not cease,
How can there be any peace?
Some people been used, abused, and then refused.
Some were killed for speaking out,
For tyrants are free to mess about.

I could not live there for long,
For I would say that they are wrong.
They might be the Nero or Hitler type,
And off the map I would be wiped.
Fighting me without just cause,
Wouldn't give me time to pause,
For tumult, oppression, are worse than slaughter,
I may have to die a martyr,

For self defence were meant to be,
Whether it is she or he.
I don't hurt you, do not hurt me,
That's the way it ought to be.
Only when oppression is gone for sure,
Mankind will study war no more.

The Ants

I watched the ants as they go along,
They are small but very strong,
If we follow their way, we can't go wrong.
Those insects are very clever,
I would like to watch them work forever.
They are a strong united bond,
For they all can understand,
Wonders they perform upon the land.
They know when it's going to rain,
The sign they show is very plain.

In summer time they all appear,
They worked like slaves just to prepare,
When winter comes they disappear,
For lots of food they have to spare,
Some human brain cannot compare.

Some live in trees, some underground,
Sometimes their nests cannot be found,
While we are searching round and round,
They are not making a sound.
The termites are clever than the rest,
I named them the danger pests,
They are the ones who hid their nests.
They do their travelling by night,
Then hide away when morning light.
They love to hide up in the roof,
Make sure your house is termite proof.
There are some kinds named pity I'm little,
They bite and burn like pepper in pickle,
But the copcops cut like a sharp sickle,
As if their mouths were made of nickel.
Some are black, brown, white and red,
But every one of them are dread.
Very clever are those ants,
Don't let them get inside your pants.

The Maxim

I came in this world unconscious,
I had no choice when I came here.
I don't want to be too anxious,
Nor to live in doubt and fear.
I want to be self conscious,
In this wide world around us.
Some are blest with great dominion,
But I have my own opinion.

If you don't want to go insane,
Let no one control your brain.
The faults of others are plain to see,
But our own, we cannot see.
Anyone who live a lie,
Should look out for that hidden spy.
Whether a woman or a man,
No one can do more than they can.
A limited time to say and do,
For we are only passing through.

Displeasing oneself, to please another,
Whether father, mother, sister or brother,
May sometimes cause a bit of bother.
Be courteous to all,
But intimate with few,
Make sure those few,
Well known to you.
Give respect to whom it's due,
Respect those who respect you.

But first you should respect yourself,
Or you'll be left upon the shelf.
If I am met with any offence,
I have the right to self defence.
When taking lives we cannot give,
We forfeit our rights to live.
Hypocrites are like old sepulchres
White washed,
At all times, they should be watched.
For whenever they're overlooked,
They use their venoms, and you are hooked.

The Bees

I was lying in my bed,
When these bees ran through my head.
Blinhaddin, Blush, Bear, Bombs, Bullets, Blood.
they ran through just like a flood.
Whether it was wrong or right,
This was what I had to write,
For it was no ordinary fight.

There was a world wide demonstration,
Pleading to save the Iraqi nation,
But our Blush'Bear leaders had insisted,
War must be the only solution,
To rid the world of Baddam's weapons of mass
destruction.
And to liberate the Iraqi people,
Delivering them from the tyrant's evil.

29

But while Iraq was well bombarded,
The oilfields were well guarded.
Bombs fell down like falling rain,
Many innocent lives went down the drain.
That was really shock and awe,
I wondered who had made that law.
When they spoke of friendly fire,
That's when I started to enquire,
Iraq sunk straight down in the mire,
This was what some did require.

But after all that were said and done,
And those battles that were fought and won,
Still no Blinhaddin, they caught Baddam,
But no weapons of mass destruction,
Only a country with vast destruction,
And there's still one big confusion,
That's why I've come to this conclusion.

Terrorists are all over the place,
Seems as if they're in a race,
To make this world a safer place,
We'll have to go and live in space.

The Unholy Matrifunny

Throughout the ages
All marriages were know as the holy matrimony,
But today many ended up costing bags of money.
At first that love was sweeter than honey,
But afterwards it just went funny.

Relationships are always breaking down,
In the country, in the town.
For all kinds of different reasons,
Minds are always changing,
Just like the four yearly seasons.
While some are chopping and changing,
Some are re-arranging.

This one was named convenience marriage,
It works like the horse and carriage,
Sometimes slow, sometimes fast,
But never ever seems to last.
Another one named pay to stay,
Which doesn't last a single day.
Another one named come what may,
Which taught the sinners how to pray,
Or how to find another way.
They made their vows to say I do,
Knowing that they were untrue.

After endless counselling and much discourse,
Many still went through with divorce.
A marriage could climb into the brain,
And cause someone to go insane.
Committing murder or suicide,
Also some to run and hide,
From those in which they did confide.

Many are enjoying true love lasting marriages,
While some continue to live like savages.
It's sad when our holy matrimony,
Becomes unholy matrifunny,
Costing millions bags of money.
We can't blame the lawyer nor the judge,
When matrimonial love turned hate and grudge.
For they neither cheat nor rob,
They are only doing a job.

The Grave

Some people thought they couldn't die,
But that was just a simple lie.
For whether we are rich or poor,
The grave is waiting there for sure,
An angel is standing at death's door,
Asking, is there any more?
The kings and queens, also the knaves,
Who lives in palaces and caves.
Where is Mary, Sam and Dave?
When they were here, they were so brave.
They went and didn't say good bye,
I sat alone and wondered why.

Lo, I cried, I'll have to die,
My mind's made up, I'm not shy,
I won't be going up the sky,
For I have got no wings to fly.
I'm now riding with the waves,

Before I join those in the graves.
This is surely what I know,
I'm having fun before I go.
Whether they were friends or foe,
I never like to see them go.

The master said this to his slave,
If again I warn you to behave,
You shall be put into your grave.
The slave was shy, did not reply,
But master was the first to die,
Which gave her a relieving sigh.
The life we have was only lent,
To whosoever it was sent,
That's why it should be well spent,
For none can show us where it went.
So both the coward and the brave,
Shall one day end up in the grave.

One God

All worship praise and glory are due to god alone,
The omnipotence who rule on his unique throne.
The living self subsisting eternal,
Never is or was paternal.
The beginning and the end,
On whom all source of life and death depends.
The knower of all that is open and hidden,
What is lawful and what's forbidden.

Some prophets were great, some were small,
But the same was said by all,
Obedience to our creator's call,
Jonah repented lest he would fall.
David was given the book of psalms,
He held firm onto the everlasting arms.
Moses was told, no other god but me,
Those with spiritual eyes can see,
This is how it will always be.

Jesus son of Mary prayed,
Our Father who dwelleth in Heaven.
The prophet Muhammad recited fatiah,
The verses are from one to seven.
None of God's prophets did preach trinity,
Nor they ever claimed divinity.
They did preach love and unity,
From the beginning until eternity.

In spite of all religious contention,
God's greatness is beyond all human
                                comprehension.
Praise the Lord, oh my soul,
We can hear the billows roll,
The lightening flash, the thunder roll,
These no mortal can control.

Angels sing songs of praise around him,
All creatures here below adore him,
Sun moon and stars bow down before him.

Worship the lord, in the beauty and holiness,
Prostrate yourselves to show your lowliness,
Almighty Creator is his name,
Mercy and justice he shall proclaim,
But those who take this for a game,
Will surely have themselves to blame.

The Journey – Part One

A happy Jamaican, healthy and free,
Nineteen sixty, I was twenty three,
And some of this world I wanted to see.
I said to my dad one day,
Here, I do not want to stay,
I would like to go away.
He asked me, where would you like to go?
Is it somewhere that I know?
I replied by saying no.
I want to go to a foreign land,
This he said, must be England.
Yes I said, you've got it right,
That's surely where I had in sight.
My father did not hesitate,
Soon he went and got a date,
He gave me what he could afford,
And on the SS Begona, I went aboard.
For seventeen days we were at sea,
The journey was unkind to me,
Nights and days I was seasick,
I felt worse than someone in the nick.
The same day that we went ashore,

An abscess gave my mouth a sore.
It was March and very cold,
Before I came here, I was told.

I was received by friends I knew,
They helped me, and told me what to do,
In those days immigrants were few,
Among the British and Irish, I was new,
I learned to stand up in a queue.
I went to the Ministry of Health and Social Security,
Where I was given surety.
For three weeks I was on the dole,
But I did not like that role.
Soon after, I was on my feet,
I started to walk the streets.
My first job was in a brick yard,
I left it for that was too hard.
I kept on searching without fail,
I got a job with British Rail.
The people were of different cultures,
I used to work in agriculture.

The Journey – Part Two

At first I found it very strange,
Soon I began to re-arrange.
My new job was to shunt goods trains,
It was dangerous when it snows or rains.
I really didn't like that job,
But it was better than to beg and rob.
Now I could manage on my own,
I felt like a king upon a throne,
I started writing to my dad,
I sent him some of what I had.
My mother died when I was nine,
My father grew me up so fine.
I loved my father with all my heart,
For he gave me a sturdy start.

Weekends I went from town to town,
For two years I wouldn't settle down.
A full enjoyment of my life,
I wasn't ready to marry a wife.
But this nice lady whom I met,
Forever I could not forget.
That was nineteen sixty two,
I told her that my love was true.
She was nineteen, I was twenty five,
Love and everything began to strive.
Within a year our son was born,
On one early April Monday morn.
Both of us was in the mood,
We were enjoying all the food.

A year later our daughter came,
The following year we did the same,
But someone didn't like that game,
And changed my name into defame.
We were plagued with stress and awe,
By my interfering mother-in-law.
She said I had a disgusting habit,
Giving her daughter children like a rabbit.
This she did not tolerate,
She had for me a lot of hate.
Our family relationship became so bad,
It had nearly sent me mad,
The sexy lady that I had,
Made me feel so very sad.
They all moved to her mother's home.

The Journey – Part Three

I was now living on my own.
The mother claimed to have opened her daughter's eyes,
But what I came to realise,
Her mother was a devil in disguise.
They didn't move in very long,
When I saw how the devil was strong.
They were all thrown out on the street,
To go and lie down on concrete.
As the sun never failed to rise,
I saw this with my own eyes.
It didn't happen in the night,
It was a Saturday, in broad day light.
They were taken to an hostel,

That was nineteen sixty five.
In those days it was like hell,
Some of my friends could tell,
How much of my tears fell,
They knew my mother-in-law very well.
One miscarriage, three alive,
That's how my children did arrive.
My eldest child was two years plus,
My second was one year plus,
My youngest was just six months old,
When they were thrown out in the cold,
They took all the madness grandmother could give,
Because they were my children,
They did not deserve to live.
She accused my baby son of catching her house on fire,
I told her she was a confounded liar.

She asked me for her daughter's fare,
That she had paid to bring her here.
I bluntly refused,
That was what had blown the fuse.

Her four children were fathered by four different men,
Who on God's earth should she admonish then?
It wasn't very long when things started to go wrong,
She and her husband couldn't get along,
And so he was forced to sing a new song.
Her new furnitures was either sold,
Or was bartered for the old.

The Journey – Part Four

Her pump and pride began to slide,
And was taken for a ride,
The same time she became very ill,
That's when she went very still.
Soon after her palace was up for sale,
Her kingdom went like a fairy tale.
She was also seeking a place to live,
Ready to receive some of what she did give.

As the days, weeks, months, years went by,
The situation of my family made me cry.
They were no longer in the hostel,
But where they went was worse than hell.
They shared a two-bedroom house with a family of four,
With no bathroom in it for sure,
Although the condition was so poor,
She begot another son, and made it four.
I'm sure I didn't sow that seed,
That one came from another breed.
The house wasn't looking very good,
There were factories nearby where it stood.
With an outside toilet at the back,
And an old shed with a big old sack.
A small house with seven children,
Nowhere to play,
They were frustrated night and day.
It was a very busy street,
But the kids kept going out to buy sweets.

One day a car knocked my son unconscious,
That made me become more anxious,
He did survive that accident,
But there was another serious incident.
A paedophile caught him on the street,
Forced him to perform oral sex for sweets.
Their mother couldn't always be there,
Nor take them with her everywhere.
I used to visit them twice a week,
But their mother and I did hardly speak.
The perverted act was well concealed,
Many years later it was revealed.
For six years they had lived at that place,
Until the council gave her a proper base.

The Journey – Part Five

As I journeyed through those years,
A mixture of both joy and tears,
Although my first love affair went wrong,
I was still young, sexy, healthy and strong.
I said, why should I live alone,
without someone to call my own.
I met some girls, very attractive,
Which made me become sexually active.
I started to have lots of fun,
I was like a bullet from a gun,
Those pretty girls I could not shun,
And they decided not to run.
Some coloured, some white, some half-white,
Sometimes I did it day and night.

The way some felt, I wasn't sure,
Some gave me gifts, some just a kiss,
But some kept coming back for more.
Pubs, clubs, parties, I was there,
I was almost everywhere.
Those days were called the teddy boys time,
When racial abuse was no big crime.
Although this place wasn't my base,
No boy could jump up in my face.
I used to get involved in strife,
But I have never used a knife.
Trouble was sometimes on my trail,
I kept myself away from jail,
To be in bed with my females.

Sex became my only hobby,
I wouldn't go out looking shabby,
I met another girl, she was nineteen,
A strong young healthy sex machine.
We didn't have a drop of bother,
From mother, father, sister or brother.
The first night I took her to my home,
There was no more cause for me to roam.
Although we didn't have much money,
I chose her to be my honey.
My other girls were full of action,
But this girl gave full satisfaction.
I just couldn't resist her charm,
We used to walk out arm in arm.
I mentioned my first love affair,
But she didn't seem to care.

The Journey – Part Six

My first love affair, my heart did bleed,
But I simply took no heed,
The next time I thought I would succeed.
We lived together as man and wife,
Another experience in my life.
Our love life was going very well,
Within four months she began to swell.
She gave birth to our daughter in September,
And another daughter the next September.
We never thought of birth control,
For sex was ruling heart and soul.
Another young family has appeared,

Our freedom now has disappeared.
With just one room, there was no space,
We tried to get a bigger place.
Although there were flats to let,
We found it very hard to get.
And also very difficult to cope,
It seems as if there was no hope.
For everything I did went wrong,
I just couldn't get along.
I could no longer cope with shunting,
So I left and went job hunting.
But everywhere I went, no vacancy,
I was on the way to vagrancy.
For over two years I was on the dole,
That's why she went out of control.
She was going out early, and coming in late,
Every day, as if she had a date.

I wasn't very humble,
So the relationship began to crumble.
I went out somewhere one day,
When she took the kids and went away.
While she was keeping out of touch,
I missed my daughters very much.
At nights I couldn't sleep a wink,
I sat up most time to think.
But this was getting me nowhere,
My children needed special care,
But I just had to grin and bear.
I enquired and found her whereabout,
And saw her coming in and out.
She was with a new boyfriend,
But I never once tried to offend.

The Journey – Part Seven

I tried but couldn't settle down,
I was moving all over town.
Soon I found another place,
Where I met another pretty face.
We were tenants in this house.
She lived upstairs, I was downstairs.
Every time I turned my music on,
It always seemed to turn her on.
Other tenants were living there,
But our landlord lived elsewhere.
We all got on well together,
Pretty face and I were like sister and brother.
But when her boyfriend was out of sight,
We used to have sex day and night.
But when her boyfriend was around,
Sometimes I didn't make a sound.

What I was doing wasn't right,
My conscience kept me out of sight.
I decided not to live alone,
I went and got another girlfriend of my own.
But all she wanted was good fun,
She arose and went before the sun.
It never lasted very long,
Again I found out I was wrong,
But still sexy, fit and strong.
My lifestyle didn't improve,
I got stuck into a grove,
So I made another move.

This was a large Victorian house,
With an attic and a basement,
In the small Heath area of Birmingham.
My room was large, above the basement.
The landlord and family were living there.
Four other rooms were rented out,
Some tenants used to argue and shout,
The landlord threatened to throw them out.
The basement was used for parties weekends,
But the police did tie up those loose ends.

The Journey – Part Eight

Unfortunately I was still on the dole,
But playing the same old sexy role.
Days and nights I walked the street,
Like a bobby on the beat,
I wanted to rest my feet,
So I went into a café and took a seat.
There I saw this pretty little tart,
At first, she was looking very smart.
I asked her to come home with me,
And suddenly she did agree.
But a few weeks later we had to part.
For when I put her to the test,
She was well below the rest.
I tried my best to keep her steady,
But the tart just wasn't ready.

I went back to loneliness,
I felt ever so blue,
And was contemplating what to do.
I didn't have much money to spend,
On no one I could depend,
But myself, I always could defend.
I sometimes used to visit my friend,
Many hours sometimes I used to spend.
We played cards, smoked, sometimes a drink,
Which helped me sometimes not to think.
But returning to this lonely room,
Was like going in a tomb.

Sex machine came back knocking on my door,
She kept creeping back for more.
She left me for this other guy,
But her soul he couldn't satisfy.
Our relationship fractured beyond the mend,
But loneliness that night made me pretend.
A night that I shall not forget,
But forever, shall regret.
I caught something from sex machine,
The doctor asked me, where you've been?S
After that, she wanted to come and go,
But I just didn't want to know,
For my moral was sinking low.

The Journey – Part Nine

After treatment, I was better,
But against sex machine, I felt bitter.

Again I went to visit my friend,
His girlfriend went out somewhere,
But she came back with her friend.
Her friend was tall, slim, with long brilliant ginger hair,
With freckles on her pretty face.
As I stared at her lustrous brown eyes,
Immediately I was hypnotised.
I just couldn't resist her charm,
My bold and lonely heart went warm.
I had just been through a storm,
I hoped that this would be a calm,
And no more causes for alarm.

My friend introduced us to each other,
From that moment we got together.
It was love at first sight,
But we worked hard to get it right.
That same night she came home with me,
Then left her parents' home, to live with me.
My aching heart, at last felt free,
My friend was very pleased for me.
She was seventeen years old,
I was nearly thirty four.
We both agreed to turn the page,
Although I was twice her age.

We lived together as man and wife,
Which made a great change in my life.
The first few months we had it rough,
We couldn't buy a lot of stuff.
Both of us were on the dole,
Our budget under tight control.
Our home duties were no big concern,
Freckles was very quick to learn.
Her parents knew that I was black,
They told her she should not come back.
Don't bring that black bastard in our breed,
But indeed she took no heed,
We were determined to succeed,
Although we were in great need.

The Journey – Part Ten

Freckles was no virgin, just like all the rest,
But with comparison she was the best.
I did put her to the test.
She was loving, gentle, sexy and kind,
Trustworthy, pretty, with an honest mind,
Jealousy was the only fault I did find,
My faults were there for her to find.
Soon after, we had a change of luck,
I got a job driving a forklift truck.
Freckles also started to work,
We had no more time to lurk.
My wages was very low,
But improvement began to show,
We were no longer dependent,
We paid up all arrears for rent,
Each week we became more independent.
Our change in life was for good,
Just the way we said it would.

But suddenly our landlord became confused,
And started throwing much abuse.
When we asked him what was wrong,
He said, we won't get along.
I said, if we've done wrong, please let us know,
If you can't say, we will not go,
Leave us, and let our love life flow,
But his resentment began to grow.
He started to pick on me,
Then he started threatening me.

We went to bed early one night,
When we saw this strange blue light,
That gave us an awful fright.
Both our heads began to raise,
We contemplated on it for days.
A week later I became very sick,
I said it was a dirty trick.
My left hip was in great pain,
I started crying and complained.
I spent seven days in hospital, placed on traction,
But soon after came a reaction.

The Journey – Part Eleven

Suddenly our landlord got a paralytic stroke,
This was certainly no joke.
He saw that evil didn't pay,
So he was forced to change his way.
Throughout his sickness, he was calm.
He got rid of all that storm.
His abuse and swearing began to cease,
And we started to live in peace.

Our relationship began nineteen seventy
One, we decided to carry on.
Our condition started to improve,
We were not ready to move.
Sex machine knew that freckles was my wife,
But again came back to wreck my life.
After what she had already done,
She expected us to have more fun.
I said, you've already got the sack,
Why are you still coming back?
Whatsoever you have to say,
Tell Freckles about it right away,
She was upset, and went away,
But took revenge another way.
My children was hidden away from me,
For years, those kids I didn't see,
I told myself, just let it be,
From sex machine, I was free.
Freckles and I went on the spree.

We went to clubs and parties weekends,
Sometimes just to visit friends.
But the weekends we enjoyed the best,
was when we stopped in bed to rest.
Two years went by, and still together,
Freckles started to visit her mother,
Between them, there was no more bother.
I kept myself out of the way,
And hoped that things would change some day.
We used to smoke a lot and sometimes drink
Those days we never stop to think.

The Journey – Part Twelve

Of all the rhythm, ism and schism,
My heart went out for orgasm.
I met another pretty girl with ginger hair,
This temptation I just couldn't bear.
She said she wanted to be with me,
I didn't say I wasn't free.
I tried but couldn't find a place,
Took her in front of Freckles' face.
But Freckles was surely not amused,
She gave Ginger much abuse.
Then suddenly, began to shout,
Telling both of us, get out.
I was ashamed for what I had done,
I realised it was no fun.
Her persistent nagging I couldn't shun.
I had nowhere else to live,
I had to beg her, please forgive.
Ginger wanted to be with me,
But it wasn't meant to be.
With Freckles I decided to stay,
And let Ginger go her way.
But it was nagging night and day,
And there was nothing I could say.

I started to play a conscious role
Got things back under full control.
Everything was going well,
When Freckles' belly began to swell.

Some months later our daughter came,
One year later, our son appeared,
Right back to the same old game.
Circumstances remained the same,
No one but ourselves to blame.
This experience to Freckles was new,
I had to tell her what to do.
We also needed much more space,
We have to get a bigger place.
We applied for a council house to rent,
But all the cash we had was spent.
We had some real hard times together,
But we did overcome the weather.
We got a three bedroom ground floor flat,
We've never had anything before like that.

The Journey – Part Thirteen

At last a decent quiet place to live,
Lots of thanks we had to give.
This was nineteen seventy seven,
One of my daughter was just over eleven.
She left her mum to live with us,
But later on, it did cause a fuss.
Freckles gave birth to another daughter,
Nineteen seventy eight,
This was her third, but was my eighth.
I decided to close the gate.
Eventually we got ourselves sorted out,
But not a lot to shout about.
The tension did release,
At last we could relax in peace.
My work place was about six miles away,
I took the buses twice a day.
I met another beautiful, near my work place,
This one seemed to be full of grace.
The first few weeks, I did hesitate,
Soon after, I asked her for a date.
She told me that I should wait.
About a month later she became my lover,
But this was kept well under cover.
Lots of secret loving we were giving,
But I couldn't tell her where I was living.
I told her I was single,
Only with her I wanted to mingle,
For she knew how to make me tingle.

We went to parties some weekends,
Sometimes a spare room at my friends,
Freckles surmised, but had no proof,
I couldn't take her near our roof.
What went on with Ginger before,
I didn't want her near our door.
Cover lover was about twenty three,
We were as happy as could be,
She was very kind to me,
She said she loved no one but me.
I said, you're the only one for me,
Again this wasn't meant to be,
For Freckles was my honey bee.

The Journey – Part Fourteen

When we had sexual intercourse,
She always scream,
But enjoyed oral like ice cream.
She also used to drink and smoke,
But never touched the crack nor coke.
We enjoyed the pleasures for nearly two years,
Before it came to Freckles ears.
While I was playing the love rat game,
Cover Lover the cat, was taking aim.
When Freckles told me Cover Lover came,
I pretend I had no shame.
I said to her, it was a lie,
But suddenly she began to cry,
She looked at me and asked me why?
I felt as if I wanted to die.
I got into another stew,
I didn't know what to say or do.
For what I did was nothing new.

Tall boy was my best friend,
The only one who would defend.
I went and told him what I had done,
The Freckles' wrath was hard to shun.
To my rescue tall boy came,
But life was never the same.
I had to swallow all the blame.

Tall boy was a friend indeed,
Whenever a time I was in need,
For forty one years we got on real fine,
Five of his kids were the same age as mine.
His kids were young when his wife died,
But he stood firmly by their side.
They grew up and went their ways,
He enjoyed some of his latter days.
He then took ill, suffered much pain,
His health went slowly down the drain.
I was at his home the day he died.
It was a flood of tears I cried.
His passing on I did regret,
But his kindness I cannot forget.

The Journey – Part Fifteen

Cover Lover was very pretty,
But she did vanish from the city,
Her memories forever will remain,
But I didn't see that face again.
I knew I was wrong from the start,
And I was breaking Freckles' heart.
Too much for her to endure,
I didn't do it any more.
I loved Freckles than all the rest,
Of all my girls, she was the best.

Soon after the affair my father died,
This was my first aeroplane ride.
Nineteen sixty I came to roam,
Nineteen years later I went back home.
My relatives home didn't expect,
I would turn up to pay my last respect.
No one could roll back nineteen years,
Nor could I hold back my tears.
My dad told me lots what he'd been through,
He went to sleep at ninety two.
I loved you father very much,
Too late to say, but here to touch.

I helped to put him down to rest,
It was my turn to do my best.
Goodbye my loving father dear,
I know some day I'll see you there.

Two months I spent where I was born,
Eating fresh fruits, sea fish and corn.
Meeting old friends, neighbours, nice girls, the lot,
Some of the days was very hot.
I was having lots of fun,
I took no notice of the gun,
I watched the setting of the sun.
Soon after I returned to roam,
I began to miss my home.
Because I've been away so long,
My love for home grew very strong.
But my family home is here in roam,
They've never been to see my home.
My kids were glad to see me back,
Some thought I wasn't coming back,
But Freckles came with verbal attack,
Surmising that I went off track.

The Journey – Part Sixteen

Just as I went back to work,
Three days a week gave me a jerk.
Cost of living went up, wages came down.
Financially I was sure to drown,
But things went from bad to worse,
Redundancy crept in like a curse.
Seven years service, six hundred pounds pay,
Nothing I could do or say,
Forget not, till my dying day.
Calamity was at its height,
Humiliations teeth began to bite,
I said, this was done for spite,
I am giving up the fight.
This has caused me great distress,
Which had brought on mental stress.
Powelism was preaching send them back,
Get rid of all those who are black.
I couldn't say I didn't hear,
It was broadcasting on the air,
With less than one hundred pounds a year,
I couldn't afford to pay my fare.
In roam I had no armour,
To protect me from this trauma.
The government had a voluntary repatriation scheme,
I went below my self esteem,
I was brought to that extreme,
By going down that murky stream.

They gave me thirty five pounds,
And a one-way flight,
A bullet that was hard to bite.
I went, leaving my family behind,
My children thought I was unkind,
But they were always on my mind.
The scheme planned to send them home to me,
But that wasn't meant to be.
The International Social Services of Great Britain,
This was how its name was written.
I wrote to say many thanks to you,
This was March nineteen eighty two.
From my journey, I came home broke,
Trust me, this was no joke.
Same time I gave up drinks and smoke.

The Journey – Part Seventeen

Where our house is built, the road is near,
The news was spreading loud and clear,
Some nosey ones came up to stare,
The ignorant ones began to jeer,
I pretend I couldn't hear,
But after all I didn't care,
I felt so happy to be there.
The people I saw in our house was seven,
Living free as if it was heaven.
Two other rooms were rented out,
For keeping clinic, and distributing food stamps.
I went through hell to get them out,
Some were just a bunch of scamps.
I tried my best to settle down,
Visiting my little farm, instead of town.
My father left it for me in his Will,
The soil I immediately began to till,
For in my pocked I had nil.
I wrote to Freckles from my home,
She replied, they were doing well in roam.
But they were all missing me,
I was busy as a bee.
It wasn't easy to survive,
I struggled hard to stay alive.
Before I could even pay my dues,
What I heard was real bad news.

Six weeks at home when Freckles died,
The shock brought on a nervous slide,
My heart and soul wished they could hide,
I couldn't afford an aeroplane ride,
But God was surely at my side,
Alone I couldn't stem the tide.
The memories of yester years,
Always been whispering in my ears,
Sometimes laughter, sometimes tears.
Despair had brought me to the brink,
But suddenly I began to think,
Learn to swim, or you will sink.
Then I heard the inner one spoke,
Life is not a yoke nor joke.
Although its inward grief and pain,
Cry no more, and don't complain,
Get up and try to use your brain.

The Journey – Part Eighteen

Brush yourself off,
Start all over again,
Show the world you're not insane.
Although my life was in a mess,
Those thoughts brought me much solace.
The last year I sat on that dole,
I was like someone dumped into a hole.
I couldn't see nor hear a soul,
My lifestyle went out of control.
I know I'm not a dunce nor lazy,
The Thatcher system was driving me crazy.
Self praise is no recommendation,
But I made reservation for self determination.
There were times when I couldn't buy a meal,
But decided not to beg nor steal,
My heart had signed it with a seal.
Though I walked through the valley
Of hardship sweat and tears,
I kept out of Britain for eighteen years.
Throughout those years my heart did burn,
But survival was my main concern,
The longer we live, the more we learn.
The half has not yet been told,
For in this book it could not hold.

Reality Rule is a unique book of poetry and events written in rhyme by the author to awaken our consciousness of the vicious and primitive past, the realities of the menacing present, and the expectations of the dreaded future that lies ahead. It offers experience to those with little or none, open our minds to many important issues which sometimes have been ignored. Gives light to those in darkness, solace to those who continue to live in fear, and new hope for those in despair.